My Sutured Mind

Poems of Healing Beyond Trauma

Find more books, buy sweet merch, and support indie publishing:
www.sterncastlepublishing.org/shop

Poems: Copyright © 2025 by Taylor Yount
Illustrations: Copyright © 2025 by Yelizaveta Bakhtina

Published by:
Sterncastle Publishing
644 SW Coast Highway #203, Newport, OR 97365
sterncastlepublishing.org
community@sterncastlepublishing.org

ISBN: 978-1-960120-22-9 (Paperback); 978-1-960120-21-2 (Hard cover); 978-1-960120-20-5 (Ebook)

Library of Congress Control Number: 2025938510

Dedication

To my inner circle: thank you for helping me put my feelings into words and for supporting me through—and beyond—my trauma. To all my doctors, nurses, therapists, teachers, friends, and family: thank you for helping me get to where I am today. Without you, none of this would be possible.

And to anyone who feels like the wounds of trauma never heal, remember that they will—with time. Wear your scars proudly; they show the world that you survived what others thought you could not overcome.

Contents

Foreword

Artivism as a Healing Practice

The word "artivism" was first popularized in the late 1990s and has since come to represent a broad range of issues that were rarely spoken of and sometimes taboo. Most recently we think of Banksy, who creates public art with messages of peace.

Historically, artivism has manifested in many ways. ACT UP, a group fighting for AIDS awareness and research was founded by a playwright, Larry Kramer. As was V-Day, a global women's movement founded by V, formerly known as Eve Ensler.

In each case, these groups brought to light the plights of millions of people and were considered taboo and even radical. Over time, the awareness and broad acceptance of their messages worked and opened up conversations that led to money for research and global education.

My Sutured Mind illuminates a concept previously ignored by others: medical trauma. Yount does this by sharing a unique perspective rarely seen in literature, the miracle of modern medicine, and a childhood at its mercy.

On one hand, lifesaving and enhancing measures, on the other the pain of recovery and carefree summers lost. We come to understand the resiliency of wrestling with this dichotomy: a loving family who wants their child to thrive, and the child who wishes they were any place other than the cold setting of a hospital.

In this debut memoir in verse, you will discover an experience that most children, thankfully, don't go through. Though often haunting, the messages here are of the author discovering her power. This book opened my eyes to a life experience I hadn't considered. I hope its truth nourishes you as much as it did me.

Kelliane Parker
Poet and author of *Down the Foggy Streets of My Mind* (Black Lawrence Press). Parker's published work centers around healing from mental illness as a result of trauma.

Preface

Taylor Yount is a resilient soul whose life journey has been marked by extraordinary challenges and triumphs since her birth in 1991—five and half weeks premature. With a rare condition where she contracted chicken pox in her mother's womb, clinically known as congenital varicella syndrome, she entered the world already facing significant hurdles. Visual impairments, deafness in one ear, and the necessity of a feeding tube were just the beginning.

By the tender age of eight, Yount had already undergone life-threatening spinal fusion surgery due to severe scoliosis. She endured craniofacial surgeries throughout her adolescence, facing each obstacle with unwavering courage and determination. At seventeen, while her peers were obtaining driver's licenses, Yount was undergoing the implantation of a pacemaker, a stark reminder of the unique path she treds.

Summers and holidays were not spent frolicking in the sunshine, but within the sterile confines of hospital walls, each medical intervention shaping her resilience and fortitude. Yount faced further challenges during her college years, taking medical leave to undergo a second round of spinal fusion.

Now, at the age of thirty-three, Yount has endured twenty-four surgeries and countless life-altering events. The medium of written verse has become a beacon of light in the shadows of disability and trauma, providing a means to navigate her healing journey. The COVID-19 pandemic, with its unique challenges, further underscored the importance of this creative outlet. Each poem in this collection is more than just words on a page; it is a window into the author's soul, revealing the circumstances and pivotal moments that led to its creation.

As readers embark on this literary journey they are guided through the stages of trauma processing experienced by the author: from the initial numbness and shock to the profound moments of digging deep within oneself, and finally, to the radical acceptance of one's reality.

With each turn of the page, the reader is immersed in the author's world, gaining insight into the complexities of living with a disability or complex medical conditions, as well as navigating post-traumatic stress.

My Sutured Mind: Poems of Healing Beyond Trauma is a creative project over ten years in the making. Through her work, Yount strives to echo the realities of those who have experienced similar journeys. Stitching together the fragments of her mind to form a tapestry of understanding and empathy.

Under the Operational Spotlight

the brightness of the fluorescent lights glares upon
the pale whiteness of the sterile cement walls,
that enclose the secluded chambers of tubes, monitors, and beds
that are as cold and hard as the walls that surround them.

the treacherous walk down the hall with the pastel checkered laminate floor,
makes my stomach churn like the process of milk into butter,
the smell of the medicated air fills the crevices in my nostrils
making me cringe at the shock of reminders this stench gives me,

and yet I have roamed these halls time and time before
following the same checkered pattern floor
it does not make it easier—
no not easy at all.

in fact, it only gets harder,
as the knowledge of realities about to unfold upon
the cold, hard, white table, secluded behind these walls,
floods into my consciousness like a tropical storm hitting the seashore.
and you try to comfort me by saying ...
"It'll be alright, it'll be okay, nothing to worry,"

but you—*you* do not know what it's like to march down these halls
with nothing on but a cotton gown, that drags across the checkered floor
as my tiny feet shuffle towards the white blanket stage
a spot light that not only pinpoints the most obvious flaws

but illuminates the imperfections that lie beneath the skin,
inspected, mechanically engineered, as to conform them to societal norms,

as if these flaws that I bear must be fixed,
breaking the uniqueness I have been born with,
only to mend my broken parts together,

molding me into a person sent out onto the journey
that society makes everyone take.

Perpetual Limbo

what do you do when you're stuck between two worlds
one below and one above
paralyzed in an endless loop
limboing in the middle,

waiting for something to pull you back or push you forward
wondering if you'll be pulled apart instead
hoping the sheer force of the never-ending tug of war doesn't split you in half,

mind fuzzy
body numb
nothing making sense
except for the few brain cells left that contain your consciousness
not knowing whether this is a dream or reality,

paranoia setting in
terrified that history will repeat itself
all while knowing in your mind there's no way this could be happening
yet the body says otherwise.

all that can be done is pray
pray that this loop between two worlds of consciousness ends
to will oneself back to reality
trying to ground yourself
to keep from soaring any further from the present moment
...than you already have.

like taking a spaceship to the ends of the solar system
only to panic halfway there
questioning if there is going to be enough of a line
tethering you back to Earth.

at this point, you know a distress signal must be sent out
your body doing everything it can to send for help
only for the safety flare gun to be mistaken as a firework,

those around you seeing the colors of light
instead of smelling the smoke that burns in the air from it being set off
praying that this residual smoke catches someone's attention,

having been here before
you wish you *could* return to the mother planet's atmosphere in time
not wanting to have happen what you know could occur next
the effects of this endless loop become greater
realizing that this tug of war of consciousness is more of a roller coaster
rather than a quick trip around a racetrack,

it ebbs and flows through your mind and body
forcing yourself to find ground
when it still feels numb beneath your feet,

the record of your body's past becomes more of a cursed compass
changing direction of where to go at every turn,

you make another distress call into the void
crossing fingers that a signal is received,

floating further out, you suddenly get jolted back
the tether back to Earth proving to be just long enough to return to reality,

the people around you having seen you drift away
realizing this time was different
your past distresses no longer seen as lit-up skies

but as the burnt ashes falling to the ground
the ground you hope they can help you land upon,

like the ashes of the flare gun
you slowly settle back down to the Earth's surface
your consciousness painstakingly taking its time
pushing its way into reality,

mind and body finally becoming one again
relieved that the past records of your existence
didn't prove themselves right
having previously torn you in two
leaving you in pieces
with only yourself to put it all back together.

after landing safely back to Earth
after soaring the solar system of panicked distress
the tug of war on your consciousness still bears its scars,

ridges of old sutures left on the surface of your mind.

The Lost Piece

I feel there is something missing
like a piece fell out of me years ago.

I should feel like I have it all:
the apartment, education, clothes, friends, family,
health, food, money...
what else could I want?

it just seems there is a need to discover something about myself
that was once present
but now has vanished.

maybe what I'm looking for is the old me that used to be,
but that person is no longer here because I have changed.

does discovering yourself mean
you realize you are the same person as in the past
...but just older?
or must you let go of that past state of being altogether?

maybe I just have to find the spark of life
that used to fuel the fire of my curiosity,
having had such wonder about the world around me.

maybe it's a puzzle piece that fell out of the box,
needing to be found to complete the picture.
whatever it is...
I hope the missing piece was put in lost & found

that way I can claim back
what I feel has been absent from myself for so long,
then try to make my soul whole again.

No One Can Cheer Up This Buttercup

why do I feel so upset recently?

it's not like something super traumatic or anything has happened
...right?
maybe because my life has been surrounded by trauma—
a little here, a little there—
my worries are different than everyone else's.

people think I'm getting depressed,
they stress out by the fact I'm upset.

but I don't fret over small things,
like whether I'll get an assignment in on time,
if someone is running late to meet up.

having dealt with so many complex things,
when I get upset
...it's not an emotional outburst.

instead, my emotions burst at the seams,
pouring my soul out.

because what has led up to making me upset
are interconnected broken wires
just stuffed inside,
waiting for ignition to explode.

occurring so many times over,
my soul is left to rewire itself,
withstanding the new voltage ready to be received—
each new trauma sending shockwaves up and down my body.

when I get upset,
it's not that I am depressed,
or that I should be "more grateful for things."

my soul is healing itself from one near electrocution to another,
leaving it riddled with scars like the ones on my body,

reminding me that even though I have been to hell many times...
...I always know my way back.

so next time, when you say:
"Oh, but you're so strong,"

you have no idea how much it takes when you have no choice
but to be everyone else's inspiration for strength.

Trying to Break Free

what do you do,
when people think you're superhuman?
has my exterior become so hardened that my insides have turned to mush?

I don't feel as strong as I appear.
maybe I'm like part of X-Men,
and my mutant power is the ability to have full composure.

I don't get how someone can think I am beyond human,
having the strength of a machine.

I am only strong with what I've dealt with—
nothing else.

it's not that I don't want to be strong,
I do... and I am glad to be.

I think it's just, I don't know how else to exist,
to be this tough and tiny but mighty.

it gets old, hearing how superhuman I am,
when all I feel inside is a world of daydream chaos.

if you looked inside...
I would be far from grounded.
I'd fly and float like an eagle going over mountaintops,
exploring the horizons,
escaping the realities of this life.

so when I hear again how I am strong or superhuman,
or I shouldn't be upset because "I've been through so much,"

why do I have to be strong all the time?
I have been strong for so long,
all it's ever done is chain me to the ground...
and all I want to do is break free.

Befriending Your Worst Enemy

how can something you've fought against your entire life
become the one thing you cherish the most?

like going into the boxing ring against Muhammad Ali,
ready to take him down,
then suddenly coming out of the match
with his arm around your shoulder.

it seems unimaginable—

as though a part of yourself is deemed the enemy,
only to turn out to be the most loyal friend you've ever had.

but this thing is regarded as a burden in your life,
so much so that everyone believes it's a burden in theirs too.

...It's the thing you've been told changed everything—

this so-called enemy,
considered untamable,
restrained between melded bits of steel and bone,
laced with miles of wires pulsating with its every heartbeat,

reminding everyone that it may now be quiet and forgotten,
but it will never be defeated.

every year, the fight goes on,

everyone saying this burden the enemy brings
is no good for you,
you must overcome its power.

You're taught to take advantage of it whenever you can,
because what good does it even do for a person "like you?"

So you keep fighting
...and fighting,
until you realize the end to this war is nowhere in sight.

One day, you look the enemy square in the eye,
daring to ask:
"Why me? Why fight with me of all people?"

The enemy then whispers back:
"Because you were the only one strong enough to see past everything... when no one else could."

...Then the final blow hits you,
like suddenly waking up from a bad dream.

Realizing that this enemy was the only thing
with you during the hard times,

helping you live through the melding of your broken pieces,
charging you back to life when you least thought you'd see another day.

as you step away from the fighting ring,
you're shocked by the restraints
...now around your own body,
only to realize that the only enemy in the ring this whole time
was YOU.

in the war against yourself,
it seems there will never be an end in sight,

...until you see that the enemy was not a burden after all,
but instead a blessing in disguise.

even the damaged parts can still be glued together,
bringing back to life the person
always meant to live as your whole self.

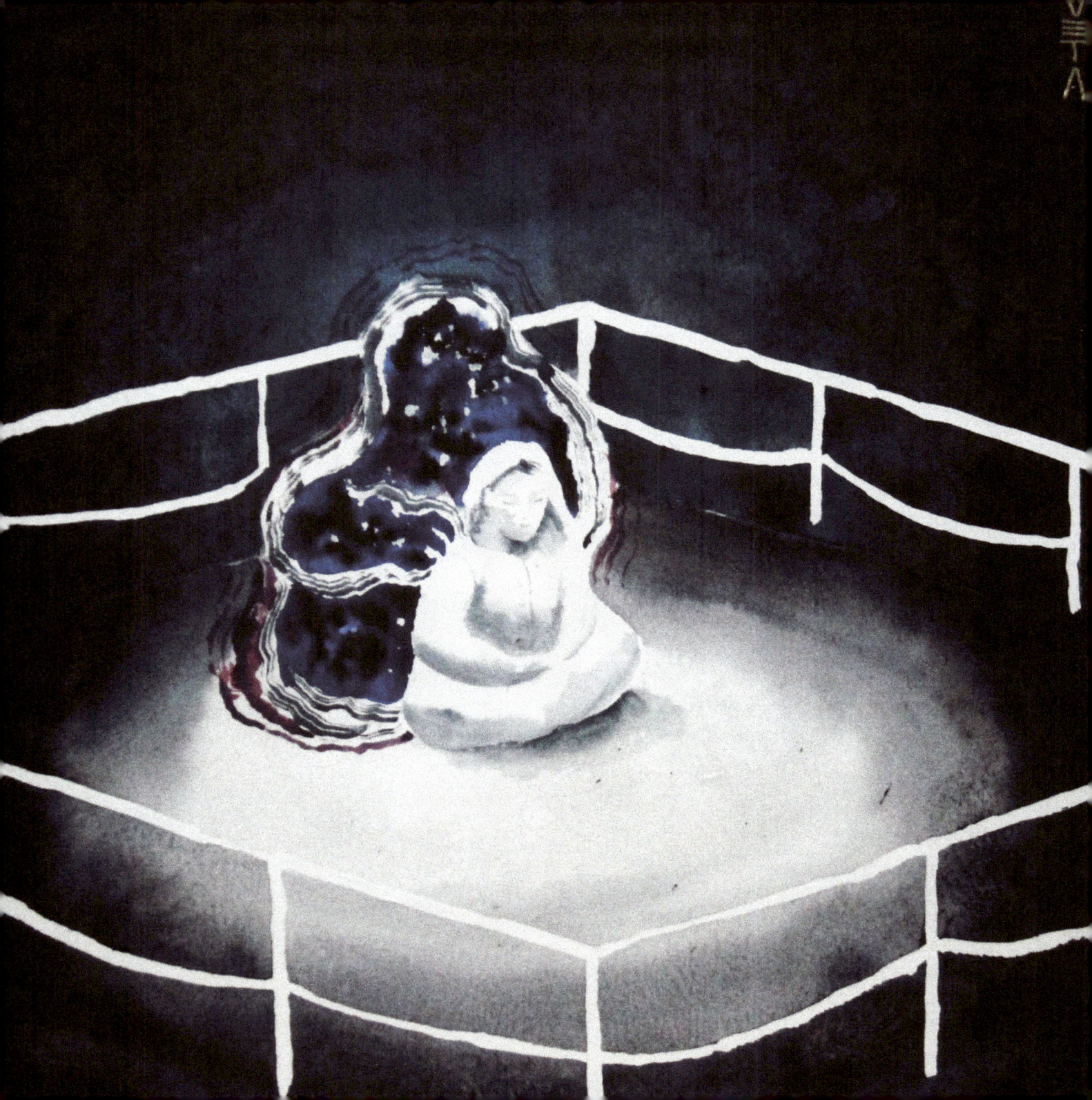

This Isn't It

they say *I hope this is the last one,*
the last one... yes, this is it.
You've made it to the finish line.

people waiting with cameras,
lights flashing,
news reporters all wanting to know: "Is this the last one?"
"The last one?" I ask mockingly.
..."There will never be a *last.*"

something that controls 24
of your 32 years of existence
doesn't just stop at *'the last.'*

it molds one's self into a different person each time.
I have been 24 different people for 32 years.

it was all so fast,
blurring like trees whizzing by a speeding car window—
too hazy to focus on what was happening inside.

when I look back, I don't even
recognize the little person who survived
all those 24 transformations.

how can you be connected with something
that has disconnected you over and over

from life itself,
making the disconnection so explosive—

launching you a galaxy away
from feeling those 24 alterations,
from those 24 years of being controlled by something,

not only changing your anatomy,
but your soul.

24 years of being put in the spotlight,
flaws cut out that were not approved of,
trying to become perfect... 24 times.

no wonder I didn't recognize myself—
never awake enough to see who I really was,
brainwashed by the antiseptic of my memories,
consumed by the trauma put on a loop running 24 times.

never knowing what's outside the white, sterile, fluorescent-lit walls,
never knowing the world out there
until you break away from it—

unplugging the tethers keeping you down,
letting the drugs that numbed the emotions of your experiences
drain out of your veins.

soon regaining consciousness,
clear enough to look in the mirror
and see who you really are.

I was told I had 24 surgeries to make me better.

now I know it took 24 times
to realize my true self still exists,
buried in the melded parts of my body—

finally acknowledging that it's okay
to be transformed 24 times,
to know there will never be *"a last one,"*
to continue on each time my body gets molded.

my soul is refined like a fine metal:
...stronger
...sturdier
...more resilient than ever before.

now it can be let out,
explore the world it's meant to be in,
toward the soft glow of the sun's light—
not the bright white of the hospital bulbs.

making its way to the edge of the horizon,
where it's always longed to be.

Fighting for Independence

I battle to do things on my own all the time,
relishing only in the glory of when I do.

then at the end of the night,
I crumble under the pain it causes,
after carrying the weight of myself on my own back.

hiking up miles and miles with a body begging to rest,
yet pushing it onwards anyway,
pretending that the pain it took to get to the hilltop was worth it
despite the grave sacrifices to get there—
sending me into a spiral of agony
that I pretend doesn't exist.

I put off getting financial assistance,
working day in and day out
at places that have valued no one's well-being,
slaving away just to prove I can make a buck.

showing I have the grit it takes,
but when I try to wave my white flag,
they threaten to put my head—and others'—on stakes.

so I keep to myself as to who I really am,
forcing me to shapeshift to appease—
just enough to fool them, as if they give a damn.

haunting me to role-play like I did
over and over through the horrors of my past self.

leaving me in a heap of despair,
trying to will myself to make it through
another day … week … month … year … as someone else,
all because I can't see how to access the life I could have.

like a movie playing over and over in my head,
the minute the screen in my mind
turns into the reality of what's before my eyes,
the dam breaks loose.

the cracks getting bigger and bigger,
until everything is on the verge of collapsing,
plunging downward toward the depths of the canyon below.

chaos flooding through,
rushing downstream,
taking everything in sight with it.

the flood becoming inevitable—
there just needs to be a way to hold on,
something to grasp onto,
grounding myself to something solid.

knowing there's still time at the end of the flood
to shoot a flare gun up into the sky
hoping that it won't be mistaken for a firework.

Stuck On Repeat

what happens when you can see the past repeat itself
just before it's about to occur?

like watching a train wreck about to happen—
time stopping right at the last second,
as if the universe is trying to show you something
that you didn't notice before.

the feelings are the same,
but the circumstances are different.

so you second-guess yourself,
thinking this situation has the same messaging,
knowing you just went through this before—
this shouldn't be happening again—
...right?

is this what it is like to witness a breakdown before it happens?

living on the verge of exploding,
returning to that ledge as you once did before,
peering over the edge,
looking down into the cracks of the canyon below.

wondering if there's another way out,
other than free-falling into it
hoping you'll learn to fly on the way down.

Finding the Missing Piece

at the end of the day
I'm the only one who can process everything that I go through.

taking care of my body
punching in and out of work
paying my bills
driving my car to every destination I deem must be reached—

everything to keep living this life.

this life that is lived so uniquely—
no simple google search,
*un*researchable even by scientific standards,
the error 404 of the human experience.

how can the validity of it not be constantly questioned,
consuming you whole,

turning you into an archeologist of your own life,
digging up the fossils of your past traumas—
any evidence of the reason things are the way they are?

then at some point, you are covered in dirt,
after chipping away all that has been deemed unnecessary,
left only with the dust of what remains of your soul,

wishing that by drilling out enough of your flaws,
all that remains is a masterpiece artifact
the final puzzle piece to figuring out why we exist.

Sabotaging Myself

what makes me deserve the nice things that I have?

finally, when there's a chance to have access to something
finally, when I begin to get comfortable with it
finally, when living an accessible life is within my reach—

yet something always comes along to remind me
that those nice things are only an illusion.

not because things just happen to me,
but because of me.
I made it happen.

all because I can't just ask for help.

stuffing everything all inside,
storing it as if there's an unlimited amount to lock away.

the terror of voicing what I need,
the worry that if help does come my direction,
will it be taken away at a moment's notice?

all that work to get help in the first place
would have been all for nothing.

so what's the point of asking anyway?

Let Me Be

it's like everyone around me is fighting to protect me from something,
hoping they are the ones that can protect me the most—
friends... birth family... chosen family... neighbors... colleagues... strangers.

everyone giving me a different opinion of how I should be kept from danger,
surrounding me with their drawn swords
waving them in front of me
stabbing in the air,
claiming to keep me safe from the monsters they say I can't see.

all I want is to just pass through,
but everyone refuses to let me go.

trying to wield my own sword,
showing them I am just as able to protect myself,
but no one seems to notice.

the only way out seems to get everybody's attention—
I must draw that sword into me.

watching everyone see me bleed out,
seeing the shock on their faces,
realizing that while they were all too busy
protecting me from everything else,

the one thing no one could do
is protect me from myself.

sometimes it's what I need—
I have to bleed just to feel what I'm feeling,
instead of people telling me how they think I should feel.

wishing everyone would leave me be
to stitch myself back up,

needing everyone to let me go
so I can fight my battles on my own.

no one can see what path they should take
if the people around you are blocking it,
too afraid to let you walk it alone.

The Month of July

the month of July is a strange time
usually supposed to be a time of hot dogs and barbecues,
but for me...

it's being suspended in a time machine,
witnessing every summer over and over,
hearing the words of my loved ones reverberate through my ears:
"oh, it's that time of year again,"
filled with birthdays, special occasions, and cherished milestones,

giving off the illusion of patriotic fanfare—
in reality, it's a stark reminder of the burnt stench that lingers in the air
after lighting off the fireworks of denial,

distracting from the chaos that still exists in the dark
that surrounds the glowing light of the lit-up sky.
for me, it was never about the parties or memories to be had.

those were just distractions from my own chaos
laid hidden in the shadows,

like enjoying a warm summer night looking up at the stars,
only to realize
that while your cousins, sibling, and friends are doing so at camp,
you are doing it in the parking lot of a hospital,
hoping to be distracted from the reality of your own summer night.

as the years go on, people get older
more birthdays and more celebrations are to be had,
watching my cousins, sibling, and friends grow up on the edges of lakes
while I grow up on the edges of the operating table.

every year the plans were the same:
the fanfare of the family parties
clouding the annual trip
down the whitewashed walls and ER waiting rooms.

maybe if the masquerade
of all the birthdays and milestones is flashy enough,
then people will be too blinded
to notice the hospital-gowned elephant in the room.

this year, however... is different—
the first time that the fanfare has been silenced,

ironically, during a time when even the biggest of parades
cannot distract people from the realities
of the place of whitewashed walls and ER waiting rooms,

the very place I spent the summers of my youth,
the very place we as a family spent those same summers
pretending it wasn't real,

lighting off fireworks up into the sky as everyone around us looked up
while I smelled the burning ashes slowly fall back down to the ground.

this year, however...
is the first time I spend this month
out on my own,

without my family,
without the reminders of the chaos covered in confetti,
without the Polaroids of the never-attended summer camp trips,

no more rehearsing the answers to the inevitable question—"what did you do this summer?"
no more putting on a face,
no more hiding the reality of why this month was chaotic
rather than patriotic.

now the month of July
can just be a month in the middle of summer,
'cause really... that's all it ever is.

Maybe

maybe the journey isn't so much about becoming anything—
maybe it's about *un*becoming
everything that isn't you.

maybe that's why nobody likes change,
maybe the transition is life's wake-up call that everything you once knew
is all the parts that you must leave behind.

maybe the reason people spend their whole lives
trying to discover who they are supposed to become
is because they don't want to face the person they'll meet
once they strip everything away.

maybe meeting the person whom they're meant to be
is the one thing that makes the journey terrifying.

maybe they have been trying so hard to become someone else
so they can just keep running away—
running away from the fear of finding out
the reality of who they really are.

because once you peel away what has become of you,
then all you have left is just you
...only YOU.

maybe that's what this journey is all about...
unbecoming someone else
to fall back into place, to become the person

that reflects in the mirror,
the person who you were meant to be in the first place.

maybe,
if you are already meant to be,
then there's no need to become anything
when just *being* as is
is good enough to continue on this grand ol' journey.

Ms. Birthday Girl

Happy Birthday!
Happy Birthday to the girl
who's embarking on a new stage of adulthood,

to the girl that decorates her life
in colorful, trendy ways,

covering up the outdated style
of feeling like this life wasn't quite the one she asked for.

celebrating each birthday
as if she's being congratulated at the end of a marathon,
as if every year is a test
to see if she can prove she'll make it through the next.

Happy Birthday,
Happy Birthday to the girl
whose life has really come full circle,

now seeing the possibilities
that were once a dream come true—
the idea that your parents once had
of you going to college parties,
living life like every other kid,
and how the doctors looked at them
like they were the crazy ones.

Happy Birthday,
Happy Birthday to the girl
who was seen by the gods in white coats, who said
that life only exists in numbers.

those numbers didn't add up—
the stats were against you.

no one expected this birthday girl would come this far,
let alone that this birthday would even happen.

Happy Birthday,
Happy Birthday to the girl
who now looks at the spot where she started,
realizing maybe she was destined to receive this kind of life.

Happy Birthday,
Happy Birthday to the girl
who was once afraid the world would see her little deformed frame,
but now she shows off her scarred body,
draped in colorful, trendy fabrics,
just as she decorates her life,

to show everyone that celebrating a birthday
isn't just a "special day"—
it's proving to the world that you can win
against everything that's telling you, *"you can't."*

Happy Birthday,
Happy Birthday to the girl
whose colorful, trendy self is what has kept her here on this earth,
to celebrate each year like she's just won a marathon—
'cause nothing feels better than to celebrate knowing
you lived... yet another year
when life itself was always against you.

listening to *'Happy Birthday'* gives the girl hope
that even she can prove life wrong
with her colorful, trendy ways
and the colorful, trendy beats she took to overcome the odds in the first place.

Defining Myself

my story is not my voice
just because it's rehearsed over and over
doesn't mean that it becomes okay
for *it* to define *me*,

being defined by the tales of what you've gone through
or the storyline of the diagnosis you've been labeled with
is not the same as being given a voice.

there comes a point when the sound of a person's voice
shouldn't be drowned out by the noise of narrating their life.

it's where all the insecurities begin—
feeling as if you are being submerged underwater,
waiting for the opportune time to pull yourself out,
out of the liquid mass that your story keeps you trapped in.

all you want is to just get out and take a deep breath,
resting your battered soul that bears old wounds,
never healing quite right the first time,
after all the fighting to bring out your inner voice.

once you reach the surface,
you long to take in that first breath,
yearning for your soul to scream out its voice aloud—

as if to shatter the exoskeleton this life story has cocooned you in,
to finally be able to break through the shell,

finding out who you really are,
piece by piece.

Stripped To Accept

how is one supposed to love their body
when every image publicized either shows you're
too fat, *too* skinny, *too* pretty, *too* ugly, *too* pale, *too* tan
... *too* whatever,

you say you stand against body hate
but at some point, everyone has done it—
judged a person, even their best friend.

so why don't we do this:
instead of stripping clothes,
why don't we strip skin and muscle,

revealing the truth underneath—
the bones and skeletons we all share in common.

'cause when we strip all the excess,
not only are we naked and raw,
we are human
in its most natural state.

when we're in that state of being,
there's no room for judgment,
nothing left to pick at.

when all the bullcrap is scraped off,
what lies beneath is surfaced—

everyone looking the same,
a new playing field for acceptance.

acceptance for the human body—
an anatomical marvel
that everyone should endlessly love.

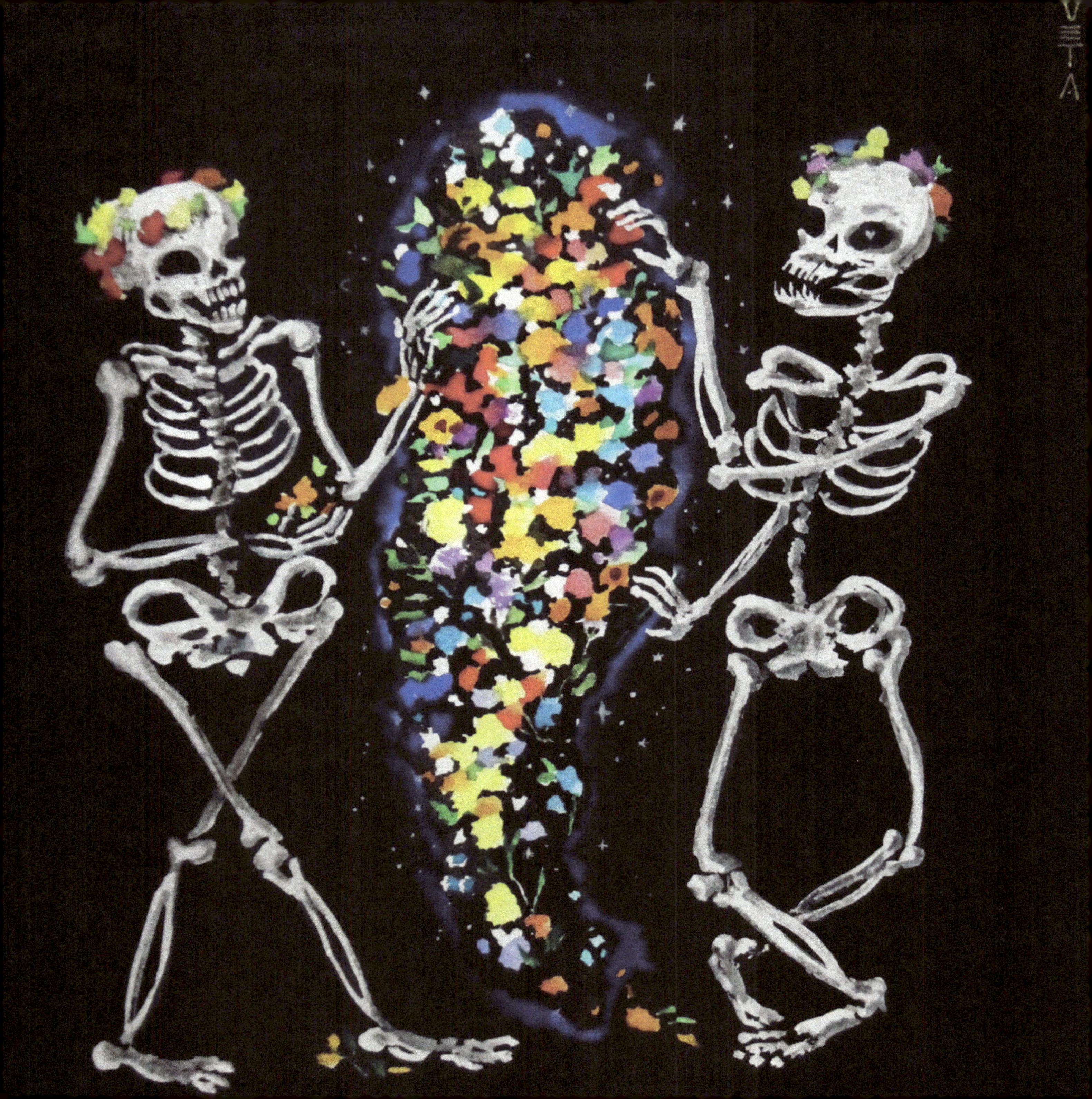
VETA

After Quarantine

what if you're afraid all of the work you put into making a life for yourself
is at risk of being blown apart
just as the rest of the world goes back to their own business?

I don't want all this effort and work to be ruined
just because other people are trying to take it away for their own amusement.

how do I know that the work I'm doing now
can last... stay in place—
just like we all stayed in place these past few months?

I don't want these little wonders that we've discovered to be lost,
pretending these lessons that we've learned
are going to be forgotten forever.

some of us have had the chance of a lifetime—
to have the world live at our pace for once,
to truly appreciate living day by day,
not filled with worry about whether we're able to catch up or not.

I wish this pace of our new world is embraced,
sharing ways of living once thought of as disabling
now seen as invigorating.

learning to thrive in a world that cherishes living on your own terms,
instead of pushing ourselves into one that breaks us down,
always stressed out and ill.

taking a lesson from nature—
that when we allow ourselves to breathe,

recovering from the pollution this chaos poisons us with,
trying to remember that, at the end of the day,
we're all a part of nature too—
all of us trying to grow tall and strong,
hoping we don't get too knocked down in the wind,
because our roots have already been tended to,
keeping us tied to this earth that made us
all we ought to be.

Starting Again

what does it mean to start again?
...does one have to upheave everything they've worked for
...start from scratch?
...can you still remain in place and make something new at the same time?

what do you do when you've gone your whole life being told you can't,
then suddenly you have everything at your fingertips,
showing that now you can—
just like those dreams you had years ago,
laying awake at night as a child,
that maybe... just maybe are becoming reality.

afraid of the truth of what is in front of you,
you trap yourself in compromising situations
over and over again,
forcing yourself to struggle from the confines of self-doubt,

almost as if your own existence doesn't make sense
unless the struggle exists right alongside you.

over and over again, you pull yourself out of the pit of despair,
hoping that this will be the last,
but in the back of your mind, you know it's only a matter of time
before you make a home of that pit again.

what if, after the darkness is lifted,
the light at the end of the tunnel is actually reached—

yet you're too hesitant to reach out toward it,
fearful that this light is not real,
that soon an eclipse will come to block it in its path,
and the darkness will slip back all around you?

how do you know that this new light is going to stay,
shining so brightly for everyone to see,
needing sunglasses to shield your eyes from the brightness
of what the future might hold?

after living on the edges of the light and dark for so long,
I guess one can never really be sure.

so for now, it'll be best to just wait—
sitting at the edge of the end of the tunnel,
observing the outside,

seeing if this new start
actually may be worth venturing into the unknown light.

Welcoming the Stillness

I used to welcome chaos into my life
greeting it like a comforting blanket,
shielding me from the truths that lie in the stillness.

when raised in the eye of a storm,
you watch everything swarming around,
standing in the spotlight, waiting—unsure how long to stay there.

learning the tricks and trades of keeping the swirling chaos in motion,
spinning it like plates on top of sticks,
praying they don't fall,
knowing all too well that if the spinning stops,
everything will come crashing down.

so I keep my post in the eye of this storm,
deceivingly making it a mini safe haven
from the seemingly obvious dangers that constantly surround me.

standing at my station dutifully,
watching the mayhem of my past destroy everything in its path,
yet all the while being too paralyzed to do anything to stop it.

but much like standing at my post,
storms can't last forever either.

at some point, these storms will end
the skies will clear with an ever-expanding spotlight

revealing the destruction left behind,
putting all the truths of the past out in the open.

the real test is not: *am I strong enough to keep the chaos swirling?*
but: *am I strong enough to face the wreckage the chaos brought?*

learning new tricks and trades to restore all that once was,
realizing that nothing can ever be completely restored.

noticing that chaos is just a blindfold,
keeping me from seeing the beauty of life that others don't—
welcoming in the stillness instead.

Being Alone

the idea of being alone is a funny thing
you see, as we grow up, it is taught to us in fear-ridden propaganda,
so whenever a time comes along that you are left alone,
it feels as if the world would crumple.

like being on the cliff, watching everything around you go under
afraid to be in the presence of your own solitude
for fear that all the haunted lies fed to you about your flaws
would come true.
so you beg people to convince you that you won't wither away
under the weight of perceived loneliness.

yet in the irony of our world nowadays,
it has come to a time when being alone is demanded.

the same fear propaganda
that kept us from experiencing the beauty of our individualism
now used to propel us into survival mode,
having to choose between life or death,
being alone for the sake of humanity.

no one enjoys being alone if it's forced,
but choosing *how* to be alone—
when formerly it was chosen for you—
can bring a sense of unexpected empowerment.

like climbing to the top of a really tall tree,
afraid of looking down between the branches,
not knowing how to get down,

only to look up and realize there's a whole new view of the world,
never before seen,
taking in all of its beauty.

in these moments—at the viewpoint of solitude—
being alone doesn't have to be fear-ridden,
like a fear of falling into the hole of loneliness
burrowing us underground once we get there
as the world has tried to convince us.

instead, let's convince ourselves to enjoy the beauty of our own existence,
and the existence of those around us,

taking in the landscape of forging your own path,
creating a new reality to being alone.

Masterpiece In Disguise

it sucks when even the only part of you
you thought could be the closest you'd get
to perfection—
to being normal—
turns out to be just as defective as the hidden cracks
riddled through the mold of your body's existence.

this body, made up of cracked clay,
held together with superglue,
remains with one untouched area—clean of scratches or marks—

only to find, underneath, there were cracks all along,

waiting to be found,
waiting for the pressure of its weight from the other cracks
...to become too much,
watching the whole body of clay
...teeter on the edge of collapse.

you frantically mend its repairs,
wondering how much glue is too much
before you start to notice the hardened globs
bulging through these mended cracks,

praying no one will look too closely,
blinded by the deceit of what others think is a Michelangelo,

when the pretend gallery artwork displaying its reality
is nothing but the rubble of a sculpture of what could be—

if only it was good enough to show off.

so you take the sculptor's place,
hoping that with every reshaping of this clay,
the cracks get smaller,
the pieces fit neater,
the edges get smoother—

making every curve of this clay body
a masterpiece of its own.

ERROR

Never Ending Season

what if the month of July never ends
the patriotic fanfare surrounded by white walls and antiseptic smells,

planning a masquerade all while it's a dissection in disguise,
slicing through the core of my soul yet again.

emotional tsunami-wrecked minds
disguised as a season of wave-kissed beaches,
challenging what I thought was real or not.

every year pretending the confetti of chaos won't return,
only for the air to be sucker-punched out of my lungs,
fighting off the inevitable.

before the anesthesia reaches my veins,
before the mask returns to my face,
before the past comes back,
before the demonic, hospital-gowned elephant in the room
creeps back through the cracks of my mind.

it's one thing to enter the operational no man's land by yourself—
what's worse ...

...watching your closest confidant go through the same thing.

them, never having trekked through the battlefield
of fluorescent lights and white walls—
you feel a call of duty to prepare them,

like a salty sergeant prepping a boot lieutenant for combat,
but only able to do so from the other end of a radio,
watching from afar.

praying they won't ever have to witness
what you keep trapped in your mind,
wishing you could take their place.

paralyzed in the fear of unpreparedness,
you frantically keep referring to your masquerade plans,
cursing that this wasn't part of it.

you're the one that gets sent out into the field,
your body the one that gets sliced open and stitched up again
...over and over.

bringing back stories to share as historical footnotes,
fables from the corridors of places no one else should see.

you find yourself having yet another month of July,
celebrating the fanfare of chaos
hidden behind the patriotic firework shows.

it's different to share it—
sucker-punched again,

not with worry,
but with grief,
mourning the reality that the middle of summer
will never be ... just that.

Life in the Field

I came into this world nothing more than a mutated human
winning the luck of the draw for survival,

raised to be revered as much of a miracle as Jesus on Easter—
pictures of me glorified in a halo of light,
as if meant to be put on an altar to pray in front of.

it's a funny story, having lived a childhood in such a manner,
spending hours, days, weeks, months in fluorescent-lit corridors,
highlighting everything in sight—
no room to hide or keep anything to myself,
learning to keep secrets in the only places I could find:
inside my body, inside the recesses of my mind.

creating a file system to give space to these secrets,
like a scientist keeping a log of the observations seen out in the field.

as I grew older, this log became more and more filled,
running out of space for these notations.

then at some point, the note-taking just stopped.

no longer enjoying the exploration of the traumatic landscape in front of me,
but I was still thrown into the field,
forced to observe, study the scene.

for a long time, I blankly stared. observations continued on,
going in and out of the white-colored interiors over and over again,

becoming so routine I couldn't tell if it was real
or if I was on a bad trip that kept repeating on loop.

a few years later, I finally had a chance to get out of this loop—
once and for all.
...so I took it!
not even blinking an eye at what it might mean.

at the beginning, the feeling was glorious
starting a new chapter in a whole new way,

pretending to never have lived my former life,
leaving my scientific observations behind,

burying them so no one could ever find them—
like they never existed to begin with,
pretending to be liberated by never needing them again.

two years later,
after riding the perceived high of a new life,
the meaning behind the decision I made
came to the surface.

I thought my newly-gained independence
was getting me that much closer to normality,

but the closer I thought I got to it,
the further it was pulled away,
falling into yet another endless loop.

as a young adult,
I thought the past had been put to rest.
how can the past come back to haunt me
when time travel is only something seen in a bad sci-fi movie?

but as if someone flipped a switch,
I was captured in a time warp,

transported to a previous time period—
same places... same faces... same smell... same hell.

the cliché "you don't know what you've got until it's gone"
rang through my ears like a fire alarm.

frantically, I began searching for those hidden notes,
desperately needing those observations
from long ago when I was in the field,
trying to gain some understanding of how I got back there,
and now—how do I get out again?

unknowingly, though... this log was buried so deep,
not even I could find it.

here I was, dropped in the middle of the war zone of my past,
with no guide on how to get myself to the other side.
so I looked in the only place I could remember.

the evolutionary survival instinct kicked in,
grasping at anything that would pull me out of this hole,
tearing apart anything that got in my way.

little did I know, the thing I was digging at was my own insides—
rearranging my inner parts like a transformer
changing from one form to another,
hoping my answer to getting out
would appear in the crevices of the nuts and bolts that held me together.

at some point, there's only so much digging left to do,
feeling as if my mission to get out of this war zone
was defeated... internally lifeless.

I began to lose hope that my observations from long ago
would ever arise,
never be able to figure out how to navigate
this treacherous landscape,

confined to these white walls and metal bolts,
there seemed to be nothing left
and feeling nothing, all at the same time.

after months in the fluorescent-lit and antiseptic-scented fields,
I was transported into what seemed like another twilight zone,
thrust back into the life I pretended to have.

that log of notes remained hidden in my body,
haunting my subconscious—trying to find them,
consuming every fiber of my being,
panicking that if my body wasn't going to reveal them
then I'd just burn them all instead,
never having the chance to encounter them again.

so I burned everything inside
anything that would get rid of any trace,
every scribble left of those undiscoverable past notations

alcohol to soak up all of the pages of these notes filed away in my brain,
cigarettes to ignite the flame, sucking it into my lungs
to smoke out any words that could utter of them,
blunts to confuse my subconscious
that the flashbacks flooding my mind were merely hallucinations,
stomach acid to disintegrate the nerves
triggered by the constant alarms those notes attempted to set off.

a year and a half later, I had then reached another point—
another chance to escape from what seemed an eternal loop.

but instead of being given the opportunity,
it was forced upon me.
not even a college graduate yet,
and my body rebelled from the inside like an old war veteran
fighting for one last attempt to be part of this civilian life.

my body suddenly broke open,
revealing all of the long-sought-out observation logs—
like a broken dam rushing through,
filling my soul with a wealth of knowledge
I never realized my body kept secret.

no longer were these notes just scribbles on a page,
but now a colorful calligraphy
illustrating the newly found purpose I could hold for my body.

being a young adult
having already transported through so many time periods,
this new purpose for my body became hard to bear.

petrified that the colors of my recently discovered logs
would bleed out my long-hidden secrets for everyone to see.

the more I tried to contain the colored ink from my logs,
the more they bled out—
running down into the street,
making people glare back, wondering
if that colored ink stream was coming from me.

my body was yearning to let the truth of my notes be shown,
proving that mopping up the colored ink
could no longer be wrung out into various buckets,
unable to keep everything neat and categorized
like the filing system of my past mind.

my colored ink notes soon etched themselves in the flesh of my body,
now bursting for all to see.

I began to make peace with my body
and the state of its existence.

instead of molding my body to the expectations put upon it,
I mold myself to the needs of my body,
letting my previously hidden secrets act as my guide.

I am still a scientist out in the field,
but now I take down my observations in bold, colorful letters,

keeping my notes within reach,
navigating newfound landscapes,
in a newfound form.

Dear Younger Self

I don't know why we exist
I've been searching for years
trying to find an answer,

something to give us an explanation as to why we're here
on this planet when others are not,
why we've been given what we got and others did not.

I know shit has been hard—
it seems the waves of darkness never leave.

just as there's a break in the clouds for the sun to shine through,
there's another storm awaiting ahead to roll right in,
demolishing anything in its path.

I know sometimes you wish the statistics of our existence also applied to us—
as if the unpredictability of surviving on this earth only implied
that we were part of the majority that didn't make it.

instead, our existence is beyond science,
beyond any reasonable logic.

I know that being given opportunities
while having to simultaneously fight for them
hasn't been easy.

it's like being born with a silver spoon in your mouth—
but it has no food on it.

you're desperately trying to get what you need,
but everyone is too distracted by its shininess,
blinded by the metallic glare to see the reality of an empty spoonful.

I know that we've fought for our needs for so long,
trying to prove why we exist—
just to give science an explanation for it.
But when something does come along to grant us that purpose,
you're hesitant to take it—

as if that silver spoon you were fed
suddenly had an overflowing spoonful of pudding,
seeming too good to be true,
too deceptive to accept—

fearing it's another trap
just to prove why the statistics lied when it came to us.

I know you've been trying to scream out,
making our voice hoarse from demanding there must be a reason—
because why else would we be allowed to be here?

we go years searching over and over,
trying to dig up anything we can find.

we've put on so many costumes, worn different masks,
trying to discover the one that'll make us look the most deceptive
to everyone else about who we are—
being just as deceptive as the science is about what we are.

I know we've been on this journey for a long time.
I know you want answers, want them so desperately.

daring ourselves toward the edge yet again,
becoming too comfortable with looking down
more times than I want to be reminded of.

I know you want these answers for your own peace of mind.
maybe then, by having all the answers,
it'll make the voices stop,
keep the thoughts from racing,
shielding out the darkness from clouding the view outside of our own mind.

but I can't give you any answers—
not in the world we are in now.

no answers are meant to be given,
not even sought after.
the only way to find answers
is to let go of trying to search for them in the first place.

I know you've always wanted an explanation for everything—
and trust me... we still do.

but some things don't have explanations,
can't be put into words,
or laid out like the results to an experiment.

sometimes the explanations are hidden—
something abstract or unexpected.

you were dealt such a difficult hand,
having been tossed into the rounds of poker with the highest of stakes
that no one could have ever prepared you for...

I am here to tell you now:
that poker face you've mastered is not needed anymore.
Instead, we use patience and strategy—
even our smarts—
to keep fighting for our seat at the poker table.

we don't need to win every hand,
but we sure as hell can gamble our way
to stay in the game.

I am here to tell you now:
nobody wanted us to find any explanations to begin with.
they weren't expecting us to—
nor to make it long enough to wish upon looking for them.
so instead, we can create our own.

I am here to tell you now:
we must surround ourselves with people and places
that give us the courage to stay at that poker table,
even when the dealer begs us to fold our cards and walk away—
because to them they question:
"why would someone with that hand want to gamble with odds that seem so low?"

I am here to tell you now:
even if our odds appear low to everyone else,
it doesn't mean amazing things can't happen.

I am here to tell you now:
if this year has proven anything,
you would see that thousands of scientifically unexplainable things
can still occur in this world... not just us.

I am here to tell you now:
proving it doesn't mean there's no reason or purpose for existing.
some of the most vital things come from existences that were unexpected—
yet had the greatest purpose for becoming a reality.

I am here to tell you now:
that we are going to work together,

making what our existence could have been
into the reality of what it can be,
reaping the rewards of every poker round.

taking back our life... one unexplainable reason at a time.

sincerely,
the person you weren't expecting to be—
and thank God you stuck around to find out.

About the Author

Taylor Yount is a disability rights advocate, entrepreneur, and poet living on the Oregon Coast. She began her journey with poetry over a decade ago, penning her first verses in the small space of a college dorm room at Santa Clara University. After receiving a Bachelor's degree in psychology with a thesis on PTSD in 2015, she embarked on a career in nonprofit work for 10 years. Yount draws upon her combined backgrounds of academia, nonprofit and lived experiences to explore the lasting effects of trauma and mental health. She uses the artistic muse of poetry to capture the unspoken emotions of trauma and transform them into something tangible. Her work reflects a nuanced understanding of the human mind, offering readers both insight and solace.

Recently, she has founded her own accessibility consulting business, while teaching at a local community college. She also serves as an ambassador for her local Chamber of Commerce, where she passionately advocates for community engagement and support. When she's not out in the community, Yount enjoys spending quiet moments writing with tea in hand and her beloved cat, Tabitha, curled up next to her. To stay up-to-date on her journey as a poet and more, follow her page on Instagram @tayloryountwrites.

Author's Acknowledgements

I would like to thank my publisher, Don Gomez, at Sterncastle Publishing for taking a keen interest in my work and representing the voices of marginalized writers. I would also like to thank my illustrator, Veta Bakhtina, for creating amazing artwork to bring my words to life. Additionally, I thank Kelliane Parker, my mentor and advisor on this journey to becoming a published poet, and for her gracious contribution to the foreword of this book. Lastly, I express my gratitude to everyone along the way for pushing me to express myself and showcase this project to the outside world.

About the Illustrator

Veta Bakhtina's work is based on her worldly adventures as well as explorations of the mystical realm of dreams and out-of-body experience. Her pop-surreal oil paintings are imbued with the aesthetic of Slavic folk art central to her culture, exploring themes of home, nostalgia, and manifestations of infinity in nature through a trans-cultural lens. Veta grew up in St. Petersburg, Russia, at the end of the Communist era and credits her exposure to uncharted nature, and tradition of heritage for much of her inspiration and working style. When not working as a traveling muralist, collecting reflections around the world, Veta can be found painting at her Creatures' Secrets Studio Gallery in Aquarium Village in Newport, OR, as well as Crow's Nest Gallery in Toledo, OR. Veta's art can be found online at www.vetabakhtina.com

Published work by Veta Bakhtina includes the children's book *The Magic Traveling Bunk Bed and the Key to Moon City* as well as the popular divination deck *The Creatures' Secrets Animal Divination.*

Illustrator's Acknowledgements

When you are fortunate enough, in this realm, as I have been, to be able to see the magic in it, sometimes people come into your life at the most opportune time. I started this project on my birthday month of November, working on the oil painting portion of the illustrations remotely as I was taking care of my ailing father.

Now six months later, I am writing this acknowledgement from the seaside jungle of Jalisco, Mexico, where I have come to let him go in the place he loved most of all. These events are bookends to this wonderful work to which I am grateful to have added my craft, alongside Taylor, my zodiac sister, who has opened up her world to me with all of its raw and beautiful edges. And Don, our charismatic publisher with Sterncastle, without whom this wouldn't be possible. Thank you especially to Kelliane at OCCC business advising for bringing us all together. And to my wonderful mother, for all of her love and support.